Travis Pastrana

By Jeff Savage

AMAZING ATHLETES

Lerner Publications Company • Minneapolis

For Taylor Savage, my daredevil son

Lerner Publications Company
A division of Lerner Publishing Group
241 First Avenue North
Minneapolis, MN 55401 U.S.A.

Website address: www.lernerbooks.com

Library of Congress Cataloging-in-Publication Data

Savage, Jeff, 1961–
     Travis Pastrana / By Jeff Savage.
        p.   cm.—(Amazing athletes)
     Includes index.
     ISBN-13: 978-0-8225-3428-0 (lib. bdg. : alk. paper)
     ISBN-10: 0-8225-3428-2 (lib. bdg. : alk. paper)
     1. Pastrana, Travis, 1983– —Juvenile literature. 2. Motorcyclists—United States—Biography—
Juvenile literature. 3. Motocross—Juvenile literature. [1. Pastrana, Travis, 1983–. 2. Motorcyclists.
3. Motocross.] I. Title. II. Series.
     GV1060.2.P39S38 2006
     796.7'5'092—dc22   [B] 2005023730

Manufactured in the United States of America
1 2 3 4 5 6 – DP – 11 10 09 08 07 06

TABLE OF CONTENTS

Travis Pastrana performs a Can-Can
Backflip at the 2004 X Games.

A Wild Ride

Travis Pastrana roared up the ramp on his yellow motorcycle. He shot off the end of the ramp and sailed high into the air. Then he swung one leg up and over the seat. Both his legs were on the same side of the bike. Still in midair, he leaned back and pulled on the handlebars. He swung backward and around in a **somersault.** Travis and his motorcycle straightened out just in time. Wham! He landed safely on both wheels. The crowd of 17,050 roared. He had just done a perfect Can-Can Backflip.

This trick is called the Lazy Boy.

Travis was performing at the 2004 Summer **X Games** in Los Angeles, California. He was competing against nine others in the Moto X Freestyle **preliminaries.** Riders in **freestyle motocross (FMX)** have 90 seconds to pull off as many wild tricks as possible. Judges award

Moto X Freestyle is another name for the sport of freestyle motocross, or FMX.

points for the tricks. The riders with the top five scores get to compete in the **finals.** Travis had never lost at the X Games. He owned four gold medals. He was the most daring motorcycle jumper on the planet.

Travis sails through the air while performing another trick at the 2004 X Games.

Travis earned great scores on several more tricks. For his final move, he tried one of the hardest FMX tricks—a 360-degree backflip. Travis zoomed up the ramp and sailed high into the air. Then he twisted the motorcycle to set it spinning. If all went right, he would turn and face backwards and then forwards again.

The crowd watches in amazement as Travis performs another high-flying trick.

Tricks with backflips are one of Travis's specialties.

At the same time, he yanked on the handlebars and leaned back. He went upside down. He continued to twirl in a circle as he went backwards in a somersault. At last, his motorcycle straightened out as he dropped toward the dirt ground. *Boom!* Travis crashed in a heap. He did not move. The crowd went silent.

A team of medical people rushed out to help him. After a minute, Travis raised his head. When he sat up, the crowd roared. Travis struggled to stand up. Doctors helped him off the track. Travis had suffered a head injury. His score of 89.60 was good enough to make the finals. But would Travis be able to ride?

Travis's mother, Debby *(left)*, stands by a young Travis *(right)*. Travis fell in love with motorcycles at an early age.

BOY DAREDEVIL

Travis Pastrana was born October 8, 1983, in Annapolis, Maryland. He grew up in nearby Davidsonville with his parents, Robert and Debby.

As a young boy, Travis loved driving machines. He got his first motorcycle when he was just four years old. His dad built a small **motocross (MX)** track on the family's property. Travis spent hours and hours speeding around the track. Soon Travis was competing in **amateur** youth motocross races.

Travis was fearless. He didn't mind taking risks if he thought he could win a race. He suffered his first broken bone at the age of seven while riding a bicycle. "He's always been a daredevil," his father said. "We've held him back more than pushed him."

When Travis was eight, he finished in second place at the National Amateur Motocross Championship in Tennessee. Officials from the Suzuki motorcycle company saw that Travis could be a star. They offered him a **contract** to be a **factory-sponsored** rider. Travis would drive Suzuki bikes and wear equipment with the Suzuki name on it. In exchange, the company gave Travis motorcycles and equipment for racing. Travis was the youngest rider to ever get such a deal.

Travis sponsors many products, including motorcycles, shoes, tires, tools, and food and drink products.

Travis soon showed that he really was a star. He won the 1992 Amateur Motocross Championship. Then he won it again the next year. In fact, Travis won the title five times. When Travis wasn't racing, he was practicing. He was always working to ride faster and better. His coach, Gary Bailey, said, "Travis is out on the track all day long. He can't get enough of it."

Travis never let his racing career slow down his work as a student.

SOARING HIGHER

Travis spent so much time traveling and racing that he left public school in sixth grade. He was homeschooled after that. He studied hard and finished his high school studies three years early. At the age of 15, he began taking college classes at the University of Maryland.

Meanwhile, Travis was doing more than just racing his motorcycles. He also performed stunts, and he competed in FMX. Travis's hard work, skill, and fearlessness made him a huge success. In 1998, Travis became the youngest-ever World FMX Champion. One year later, he made a big splash at the X Games in San Francisco, California. Nearly 250,000 people watched him perform a thrilling routine.

Travis and his 199 bike take the lead at an MX race. Travis ruled the sport for years.

To finish the show, Travis roared his bike straight for the **pier** above San Francisco Bay. Racing at top speed, he launched 100 feet into the air. Then he kicked his motorbike away and splashed into the water. The crowd went wild. A boat was there to pick him up and bring him back to shore. The ESPN television network hired a crew to pull Travis's motorcycle up from the bottom of the bay. He earned the gold medal with an amazing score of 99 out of 100.

Travis thrilled the crowd with his daring jump into San Francisco Bay at the 1999 X Games.

Travis performs a high-flying backflip.

By this time, Travis was unbeatable in FMX. In 1999, he won the freestyle competition at the first-ever **Gravity Games.** In the next few years, he went on to win several more gold medals in the X Games and Gravity Games.

In 1999, Travis appeared on *The Late Show with David Letterman.* He jumped his motorcycle from one ramp to another on a New York City street and crashed into a fire hydrant. He broke his collarbone but didn't tell anyone. He won a motocross race one week later.

Travis burst onto the Supercross scene in 2000. He quickly showed himself to be one of the best racers.

And Travis kept on winning motorcycle races too. In 2000, he won the 125cc National Motocross Championship. That same year, he started racing in **Supercross** events. In his **rookie** season, he won three Supercross races. He was the third-best Supercross rider and won the Rookie of the Year Award.

In 2000, Travis competed in an event known as the Motocross des Nations. Travis was the youngest rider ever to represent the United States in this world-famous event. Team USA won the gold medal.

Travis's success earned him the nickname Wonder Boy. He became famous, and his face appeared on the cover of magazines. Travis also became rich. His main sponsors—Suzuki, Acclaim, and No Fear—paid him extra money if he finished in the top 3 in a race. Travis earned as much as $40,000 a week. But Travis has paid a high price for his success. He has had many crashes and spent a lot of time in the hospital.

Travis kicks his legs out in a move called the Indian Air.

CRASHES

Flying 100 feet through the air would frighten anyone. "I scare myself every day I get on a motorcycle," Travis says. But Travis tries to stay confident. And he knows that having no fear can be dangerous.

In his lifetime, Travis has suffered 30 broken bones and nine head injuries. He has broken bones in his foot, ankle, leg, wrist, arm, hands, fingers, hips, and back. He has also broken his kneecap and elbow. Doctors are amazed that Travis can still walk. Travis's parents support his racing. But they admit that it is hard. "I don't like watching," his father says. "It's not safe."

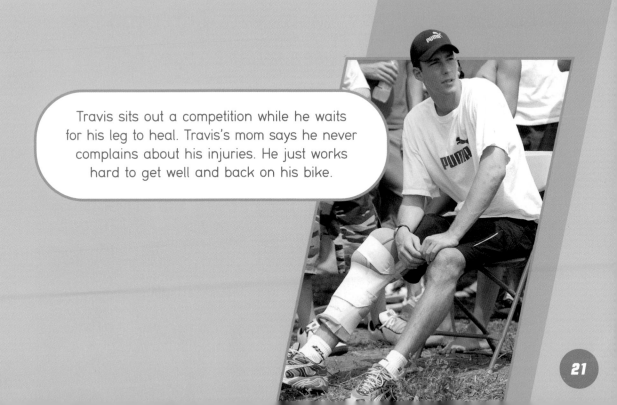

Travis sits out a competition while he waits for his leg to heal. Travis's mom says he never complains about his injuries. He just works hard to get well and back on his bike.

Once after Travis had gotten in a bad accident, his mother said, "I hate it. I wish he would give it up. But he loves it."

Travis's mother films his jumps on a video camera. For Travis, the crashes are a chance to learn and improve. He often watches his routines on video so he can perform them better. But when Travis crashes, his mother often drops the camera and runs to check on him. Travis will say, "Mom, why didn't you get the wreck, so we can see what happened?"

Travis with his parents, Debby (left) and Robert (right).

Travis's bike breaks into pieces after a hard landing.

Debby Pastrana was filming when Travis had his worst crash ever. It happened at Lake Havasu, Arizona. Travis landed short on a 120-foot jump. He hit the ground so hard that his head slammed into his stomach. He hurt his back very badly. "I thought he was dead," his father said.

In 2001, Travis learned how to skydive. He was preparing for an amazing stunt in the Grand Canyon. With a camera crew filming him, Travis rode his bike off a ramp into the canyon. He did a backflip, pushed away the bike, and parachuted into the 2,000-foot gorge.

But when Travis awoke in the hospital, he said to his mother, "Do you have it on film?" Travis spent three weeks in the hospital and three months in a wheelchair. Yet he never thought about quitting. "The whole time I was recovering," Travis said, "I was thinking what tricks to do next."

Travis's exciting career has earned him fame, fortune, and fun.

LEAVING HIS MARK

Travis has survived a lifetime of crashes and has become a millionaire. He lives in a huge house in Annapolis, Maryland. One of the rooms in his home is filled with trophies.

Travis pulls off a backflip at the 2005 Summer X Games. He won a gold medal at the event.

But Travis cannot win every event. His streak of X Games Moto X Freestyle victories ended in 2004. His injury in the preliminaries kept him from trying his most daring tricks in the finals. Travis finished second to Nate Adams.

In 2005, a broken wrist kept Travis from racing Supercross. He tried to race while wearing a cast, but he couldn't control his bike. So he had to skip the season. But in August, he bounced back to win the 2005 X Games Moto X Freestyle gold medal.

Some extreme sports athletes like to act tough. They listen to heavy metal music and have tattoos and body piercings. Travis is different. He doesn't look or act like a troublemaker. "It's hard when your friends try to get you to do things that you know are wrong," Travis says. "If your friends are doing things you don't want to do, it's time to find new friends."

Travis's good image has helped him and made him popular. Companies love having him in their ads. His image is on trading cards, toys, puzzles, and action figures. Travis even has a video game named after him.

"In freestyle, you are more artist than athlete," says Travis. "It's complete expression. You create tricks in your mind."

Rally cars are Travis's newest source of thrills. Rally cars race on off-road courses and on city streets.

Travis keeps trying new things. He has started racing **rally cars.** "If it has a motor and wheels," he says, "count me in." No matter the sport, Travis will always want the thrill of a challenge. "My strengths and weaknesses are the same," he explains. "I've got the willingness and stupidity to try anything. If I think it's even remotely possible, I'll do it."

Selected Career Highlights

2005 Won fifth Summer X Games Moto X
Freestyle (FMX) gold medal
Competed for first time in national
rally car racing

2004 Won Summer X Games Moto X Freestyle
silver medal

2003 Won fourth Summer X Games Moto X
Freestyle gold medal

2002 Won Summer Gravity Games gold medal

2001 Won third Summer X Games Moto X
Freestyle gold medal
Won 125cc East Supercross Series
championship
Named ESPN Motocross Rider of the Year

2000 Youngest rider ever to represent the United States in Motocross
des Nations
Won 125cc National Motocross Championship
Named AMA Supercross Rookie of the Year
Won second Summer X Games Moto X Freestyle gold medal

1999 Won Horizon Award as top amateur motocross racer
Won first Summer X Games Moto X Freestyle gold medal
Won Summer Gravity Games gold medal and doubles gold medal

1998 Won World FMX Championship

Glossary

amateur: someone who receives no prize money for playing in a sporting event

contract: a written agreement

factory-sponsored: supported with money or equipment by a motorcycle manufacturer

finals: the last round of competition. The winner of the finals is the champion.

freestyle motocross (FMX): a contest in which riders perform daring midair tricks on motocross motorcycles. FMX is sometimes known as Moto-X Freestyle.

Gravity Games: a series of extreme sports competitions started in 1999

motocross (MX): a motorcycle race, often involving 40 or more riders, staged outdoors on a dirt track with hills and wide turns

pier: a structure that extends from land out over water

preliminaries: the first round of competition. In FMX, the top-scoring riders from the preliminaries move on to the finals.

rally cars: cars that compete one at a time in timed races, often on dirt roads

rookie: a first-year rider

somersault: a forward or backward movement where a person turns end over end in a complete revolution

Supercross: a motorcycle race, normally limited to 25 riders, held in a stadium on a short track marked by large jumps and tight turns

X Games: a series of extreme sports competitions started in 1995 by ESPN television network, featuring the world's top extreme athletes

Further Reading & Websites

Armentrout, David, and Patricia Armentrout. *Travis Pastrana*. Vero Beach, FL: Rourke Publishers, 2005.

Mahaney, Ian F. *Travis Pastrana: Motocross Champion*. New York: PowerKids Press, 2005.

Poolos, J. *Travis Pastrana: Motocross Superstar*. New York: Rosen Publishing Group, 2005.

The Official Site of the X Games
http://www.expn.go.com
The ESPN network's website for the X Games provides fans with results of all competitions, as well as features and information on extreme athletes.

Sports Illustrated for Kids
http://www.sikids.com
The *Sports Illustrated for Kids* website covers all sports, including freestyle motocross.

Travis's Website
http://www.travis-pastrana.com
This is Travis's official website, featuring trivia, photos, race results, news, and other information about Travis.

Index

Photo Acknowledgments

The images in this book are used with permission of: © Ryan Mahoney-Photocross.net, pp. 4, 6, 7, 25; © Tony Donaldson/Icon SMI, pp. 8, 9, 14, 21, 26; © Action Photos/Racer X Illustrated, p. 11; © Diane Moore/Icon SMI, p. 15; © Eric Johnson/Racer X Illustrated, p. 16; © Larry Kasperek/NewSport/CORBIS, p. 17; © Jeff Kardas/Getty Images, p. 18; © Steve Bruhn, pp. 20, 29; © Davey Coombs/Racer X Illustrated, p. 22; © Raymond Gundy/Racer X Illustrated, p. 23; © Subaru of America, Inc./PR Newswire Photo Service, p. 28.

Cover image: © Streeter Lecka/Getty Images.